MORE GROSS JOKES

From the Editors at Tangerine Press

Illustrations by Buck Jones

Designed by Deena Fleming

Copyright© 2005 Scholastic Inc

an imprint of

SCHOLASTIC

www.scholastic.com

Scholastic and Tangerine Press and associated logos are trademarks of Scholastic Inc.

Published by Tangerine Press, an imprint of

Scholastic Inc; 557 Broadway; New York, NY 10012

10 9 8 7 6 5 4 3 2 1
ISBN 0-439-85097-5
Printed and bound in China

SICK AND TWISTED

DOCTOR, HOW DO I STOP MY NOSE FROM RUNNING?

Stick out your foot and trip it.

WHAT'S THE PERFECT CURE FOR DANDRUFF?

Baldness!

IF BUTTERCUPS ARE YELLOW, WHAT COLOR ARE HICCUPS?

Burple.

WHAT DID THE SKIER SAY WHEN HER FRIEND SAID HER NOSE WAS RUNNING?

No it's snot!

WHAT DO YOU CALL TWO MEDICINE MEN?

Pair-a-medics!

DOCTOR: "I CAN'T DO ANYTHING ABOUT YOUR CONDITION. I'M AFRAID IT'S HEREDITARY."

Patient: "In that case, send the bill to my parents."

HOW DO YOU PREVENT A SUMMER COLD?

Catch it in the winter!

YOUR COUGH SOUNDS BETTER TODAY.

It should, I practiced all night!

WHAT KIND OF ILLNESS DID THE KARATE INSTRUCTOR HAVE?

Kung flu!

WHY DON'T DINOSAURS PICK THEIR NOSES?

Because they don't know what to do with a 20 pound booger.

WHATS BLACK AND WHITE AND GREEN?

A zebra with a runny nose.

DID YOU HEAR ABOUT THE MAN WHO LOST HIS WHOLE LEFT SIDE?

He's all-right now!

WHERE DO DOCTORS GO ON VACATION?

Ill-inois!

WHY DID THE KING GO TO THE DENTIST?

To get his teeth crowned!

DOCTOR, YESTERDAY I THOUGHT I WAS A PIG.

Well, how are you today?

SWINE, THANKS!

WHAT DID THE FRENCH MAN SAY AFTER GETTING CAUGHT IN THE RAIN?

Eiffel a cold coming on!

WHY DID THE SICK SKUNK STAY IN BED FOR A WEEK?

Doctors odors.

WHAT WAS WRITTEN ON THE HYPOCHONDRIAC'S TOMBSTONE?

"I told you I was sick!"

WHY DID THE HACKER GIVE HIS COMPUTER A BOX OF TISSUES?

Because it had a nasty virus!

WHAT DO YOU GIVE A COWBOY WITH A COLD?

Cough stirrup.

HOW DO BABIES GET TO SCHOOL?
On a drool bus.

WHAT DO YOU CALL A SPY WITH A RUNNY NOSE?
A dribble agent.

WHY DID THE NOSE CROSS THE ROAD?
It got tired of being picked on.

YOU CAN PICK YOUR NOSE AND YOU CAN PICK YOUR FRIENDS—
BUT YOU CAN'T PICK YOUR FRIEND'S NOSE.

DID YOU EVER SEE THE MOVIE "CONSTIPATED?"

It never came out!

WHAT LOSES ITS HEAD IN MORNING AND GETS IT BACK AT NIGHT?

Your pillow.

DID YOU JUST PICK YOUR NOSE?

No, I've had it since the day I was born!

DID YOU HEAR THE ONE ABOUT THE GIANT WHO THREW UP?

It's all over town.

WHAT'S GREEN AND SINGS?

Frank Snottra!

WHAT DID ONE EYE SAY TO THE OTHER?

Between you and me... something smells!

HOW MANY KNEES DO YOU HAVE?

Your right knee, your left knee, and your 2 kid-knees!

WHAT'S DUMB?

Directions on toilet paper.

WHAT'S DUMBER THAN THAT?

Reading them.

EVEN DUMBER?

Reading them and learning something.

DUMBEST OF ALL?

Reading them and having to correct something that
you've been doing wrong.

DID YOU KNOW THAT DIARRHEA IS HEREDITARY?
Yeah, it runs in the jeans!

WHO ALWAYS STEALS THE SOAP IN THE BATHROOM?
The robber ducky!

WHAT DO YOU CALL A SICK EAGLE?
Ill-eagle!

WHY DID THE COMPUTER GO TO THE DOCTOR?
It had a virus!

WHAT DO YOU CALL A CHILD'S KNEES?

Kid-neys!

WHY DID ALL THE GIRL MUSHROOMS WANT TO GO OUT WITH THE GUY MUSHROOM?

Because they knew that he was a fungi!

WHAT DID THE GIRL DO AFTER SHE DRANK EIGHT SODAS?

She burped 7UP!

HOW DID THE BOY GET THE EGYPTIAN FLU?

He caught it from his mummy!

HOW DO VAMPIRE FOOTBALL PLAYERS GET THE MUD OFF?

They all get in the bat tub.

HOW DO YOU MAKE A TISSUE DANCE?

Put a little boogie in it!

WHAT DID ONE TONSIL SAY TO THE OTHER TONSIL?

Get dressed, the doctor is taking us out tonight!

WHAT CAN YOU CATCH, BUT NOT THROW?

A cold!

WHAT DID THE BANANA SAY TO THE DOCTOR?

"I'm not peeling very well!"

WHAT HAS A BOTTOM ON ITS TOP?
Your leg!

WHY WERE THE TEACHER'S EYES CROSSED?
She couldn't control her pupils.

WHERE DID THE SHIP GO WHEN IT WAS SICK?
It went to see a dock!

WHY ARE BOOGERS DIFFICULT DINERS?
Because they're so picky!

WHAT KIND OF BUTTON WON'T UNBUTTON?
A belly button!

WHY ARE FALSE TEETH LIKE STARS?
Because they come out at night!

WHY CAN'T A NOSE BE TWELVE INCHES LONG?
Because then it would be a foot!

WHY WAS THE NOSE TIRED?
Because it kept running!

WHAT DO BASKETBALL PLAYERS AND BABIES HAVE IN COMMON?
They both dribble!

WHAT DID THE NUT SAY WHEN IT SNEEZED?
Cashew!

WHAT HAPPENS IF YOU EAT YEAST AND SHOE POLISH?
Every morning you'll rise and shine!

WHAT HAPPENED TO THE WINDOW WASHER WHO INHALED?

He got a pane in his stomach!

WHAT NAILS DO CARPENTERS HATE TO HIT?

Fingernails!

WHY ARE FARMERS SO MEAN?

Because they pull ears off corn!

WHY DID THE BOY WEAR DIAPERS TO THE BIRTHDAY PARTY?

Because he's a party-pooper!

WHAT DO YOU GET WHEN YOU ADD 13 HOSPITAL PATIENTS AND 13 HOSPITAL PATIENTS?

Twenty sicks!

DOCTOR, I'VE JUST BEEN BITTEN ON THE LEG BY A WEREWOLF.

Did you put anything on it?

NO, HE SEEMED TO LIKE IT AS IT WAS.

DOCTOR, I'M ON A DIET AND IT'S MAKING ME GRUMPY. YESTERDAY I BIT SOMEONE'S EAR OFF.

Oh dear, that's a lot of calories!

DOCTOR, I KEEP THINKING I'M A SNAKE ABOUT TO SHED ITS SKIN.

Why don't you go behind the screen and slip into something more comfortable.

18

DOCTOR, YOU'VE GOT TO HELP ME – I KEEP DREAMING OF BATS, CREEPY-CRAWLIES, DEMONS, GHOSTS, MONSTERS, VAMPIRES, WEREWOLVES, AND YETIS . . .

Interesting...do you always dream in alphabetical order?

DOCTOR, I SWALLOWED A BONE.

Are you choking?

NO, I REALLY DID!

DOCTOR, MY BROTHER SWALLOWED A ROLL OF FILM!

Hmmmm. Let's hope nothing develops.

DOCTOR, I KEEP DREAMING THERE ARE GREAT, GOOEY, BUG-EYED MONSTERS PLAYING TIDDLEDYWINKS UNDER MY BED. WHAT SHALL I DO?

Hide the tiddledywinks.

A MONSTER WENT TO SEE THE DOCTOR BECAUSE HE KEPT BUMPING INTO THINGS, AND THE DOCTOR TOLD HIM HE NEEDED GLASSES. "WILL I BE ABLE TO READ WITH THEM?" ASKED THE MONSTER.

"Yes," the doctor said.

"THAT'S AMAZING!" THE MONSTER SAID, "I DIDN'T KNOW HOW TO READ BEFORE."

DOCTOR, HOW LONG CAN ONE LIVE WITHOUT A BRAIN?

That depends. How old are you?

DOCTOR, I KEEP SEEING AN INSECT SPINNING AROUND.

Don't worry, it's just a bug that's going around!

DOCTOR, MY SISTER HAS SWALLOWED MY PEN, WHAT SHOULD I DO?

Use a pencil till I get there.

DOCTOR, I'VE GOT BAD TEETH, STINKY BREATH, AND SMELLY FEET.

Sounds like you've got Foot and Mouth Disease!

GROSSEST THINGS OVERHEARD IN A RESTROOM STALL:

- "Oh no! My glass eye!"
- "Now how did THAT get there?"

GROSSEST "BE-RIGHT-BACK" INSTANT MESSAGES:

- "Nature is calling and I'm answering!"
- "It's that time of week again. I'm in the shower."
- "When you got to go, you got to go."

ANIMAL CRACKERS

WHAT HAPPENS WHEN YOU CROSS A CAT AND A FISH?

You get a purr-anha!

WHAT DO YOU FEED A CAT THAT HOWLS ALL NIGHT LONG?

Tune-a-fish!

WHAT LEAVES FOOTPRINTS ALL OVER THE OCEAN FLOOR?

A sole fish!

HOW DO YOU MAKE A SNAKE CRY?

Take away its rattle!

WHERE SHOULDN'T A DOG GO SHOPPING?
A flea market!

**WHAT DO YOU GET WHEN YOU CROSS A SKUNK
WITH A TEDDY BEAR?**
Winnie the PYEW!

WHY DID THE BEARS GET GROUNDED?
Because they growled at their mother!

**HOW DO YOU KNOW WHEN A DOG HAS
BEEN NAUGHTY?**
It leaves a little poodle on the carpet!

WHAT'S GRAY AND SPINS AROUND AND AROUND?

An elephant stuck in a revolving door.

WHAT DO YOU CALL A BEAR WITH NO TEETH?

A gummy bear.

WHAT DID ONE FISH SAY TO THE OTHER?

If you keep your mouth closed, you won't get caught!

WHAT'S A FISH'S WORST DAY?

Friday.

WHAT DO YOU GET WHEN YOU CROSS A BLUE CAT AND A RED PARROT?

A purple carrot!

WHAT DID THE BOY OCTOPUS SAY TO THE GIRL OCTOPUS?

Can I hold your hand hand hand hand hand hand hand hand?

WHAT DO YOU GET WHEN YOU CROSS AN OCTOPUS AND A HUNGRY SHARK?

An octagon!

WHAT DOES A TRICERATOPS SIT ON?

Its Tricera-bottom!

WHAT DO YOU CALL A FISH WITH NO EYE?

A f-sh.

WHAT DO YOU GET WHEN YOU CROSS A SHEEP AND A PORCUPINE?

An animal that can knit its own sweaters.

WHAT DO YOU GET WHEN YOU CROSS A BANK WITH A SKUNK?

Dollars and scents!

DO YOU THINK IT'S HARD TO SPOT A LEOPARD?

No, they come that way.

WHY DID THE FROG SAY MEOW?

He was learning a foreign language.

WHY DOES A FROG STAND IN THE OUTFIELD?

So that he won't miss a fly.

WHAT DO YOU DO IF A RHINO CHARGES YOU?

Take away his credit card!

WHAT DO YOU CALL A FROZEN CAT?
A catsicle.

WHY AREN'T FISH GOOD TENNIS PLAYERS?
They don't like getting close to the net.

WHAT DO YOU CALL LASSIE AFTER SHE SAT BY THE FIRE?
A hot dog!

WHY DO GIRAFFES HAVE LONG NECKS?
Because they have smelly feet!

WHAT DID THE PIG SAY WHEN THE MAN GRABBED HIM BY THE TAIL?

That's the end of me...

WHAT DO LIONS CALL ANTELOPES?

Fast food!

WHY DO FISH LIVE IN SALT WATER?

Because pepper makes them sneeze!

WHAT IS A SHARK'S FAVORITE GAME?

Swallow the leader!

WHAT IS SNAKE'S FAVORITE SUBJECT?

Hiss – tory

WHY CAN'T YOU PLAY JOKES ON SNAKES?

Because you can never pull their legs.

WHAT HAPPENED WHEN THE CAT SLEPT UNDER THE CAR?

She woke up oily the next morning!

WHAT ANIMAL IS THE COOLEST IN THE SWAMP?

The hip-o!

WHY SHOULD YOU NEVER WARM UP TO A SNAKE?

Because they're cold-blooded.

WHY DID THE TWO BOA-CONSTRICTORS HANG OUT TOGETHER?

Because they had a crush on each other.

WHAT DO YOU GET WHEN YOU CROSS A VINE WITH A RATTLE SNAKE?

Poison ivy!

WHAT DID THE SHARK SAY TO THE SURFER?

I just stopped by for a bite!

WHAT DID THE SHARK SAY WHEN IT SAW THE SURFERS PULL UP IN THEIR CAR?

Look, canned food!

WHAT KIND OF NUTS DO TOADS LIKE?

Croak-o-nuts!

WHAT DO YOU SAY TO A FROG WHO'S RUNNING LATE?

Hop to it!

WHAT DO YOU CALL A SLEEPING LIZARD?

A calm-eleon!

WHAT DO YOU GET WHEN YOU CROSS A SQUID WITH A CAT?

An octo-pus!

WHAT TWO ANIMALS GO EVERYWHERE YOU GO?

Your calves.

WHAT DO YOU GET WHEN YOU PUT A SNAKE IN AN ORCHESTRA?

A boa conductor!

WHAT ANIMAL ALWAYS HAS A SORE THROAT?

A horse!

WHAT DO YOU GET IF YOU CROSS RABBITS AND TERMITES?

Bugs bunnies.

WHAT DO YOU CALL FISHING WHEN YOU DON'T CATCH ANY FISH?

Drowning worms!

WHAT DO YOU GET WHEN YOU CROSS A COW WITH A RABBIT?

Hare in your milk!

WHERE DOES A BIRD GO WHEN IT LOSES ITS TAIL?

To a retail store.

WHAT DID THE FROG SAY TO THE SAD TOAD?
Warts on your mind?

WHAT DO YOU GET WHEN YOU PUT A SNAKE IN A DRINKING CUP?
A snake in the glass!

WHAT DO YOU CALL A PIG WITH THREE EYES?
A piiig.

HOW DO SHEEP FEEL ABOUT WOOLEN UNDERWEAR?
Freezing!

WHAT DOES A KITTEN SAY ABOUT HUNTING GIANT RODENTS?

I'd rat-her not!

WHAT DO YOU GET WHEN YOU CROSS A FROG AND A BUNNY?

A ribbit rabbit!

BABY SNAKE: "Mom, are we poisonous?"
MOMMY SNAKE: "Yes, why do you ask?"
BABY SNAKE: "Because I just bit my tongue."

WHAT DOES A SKUNK CALL ITS FAVORITE RECIPE BOOK?

A best smeller!

WHAT HAPPENED WHEN THE COW JUMPED OVER THE BARBED WIRE FENCE?

It was an udder catastrophe!

WHAT DOES AN AARDVARK LIKE ON ITS PIZZA?

Ant-chovies.

WHY SHOULD YOU NEVER TELL YOUR PIG FAMILY SECRETS?

Because it is bound to squeal!

WHAT DO YOU SAY TO A BROWN CHAMELEON?
Lighten up!

WHAT IS WRITTEN ON A SIGN THAT POINTS TO A BAT CAVE?
Hang in there.

WHAT DO YOU CALL A COW WITH A TWITCH?
Beef jerky!

WHAT KIND OF SANDWICH IS GREEN AND BOUNCES?
A frog sandwich!

HOW CAN A PET FROG SPEND ALL DAY IN THE RAIN AND NOT GET A SINGLE HAIR WET?

That's easy—frogs don't have hair!

WHY DOESN'T A SNAKE USE UTENSILS AT THE TABLE?

Because he already has a forked tongue!

WHAT DID THE GIRL SAY TO THE REPTILE THAT SURPRISED HER?

Don't snake up on me!

WHAT KIND OF DOGS ALWAYS GET INTO FIGHTS?

Boxers!

WHY DID THE FISHERMAN THROW PEANUT BUTTER INTO THE OCEAN?

To go with the jellyfish!

WHY DO CATS HAVE FUR BALLS?

Because they love a good gag!

WHAT DO YOU CALL AN INJURED RHINO?

A rhino-sore-us.

HAVE YOU HEARD THE SKUNK JOKE?

You don't want to; it really stinks!

HOW DO YOU MAKE A SKUNK STOP SMELLING?
Hold its nose!

**HOW MANY SKUNKS DOES IT TAKE TO MAKE
A BIG STINK?**
A phew!

**WHAT DID THE JUDGE SAY WHEN A SKUNK ENTERED
THE COURTROOM?**
Odor in the court!

WHAT DO YOU CALL A FLYING SKUNK?
A smell-icopter.

WHAT DO YOU GET WHEN YOU CROSS
A BEAR AND A SKUNK?

I don't know, but it can easily get a seat on the bus!

WHAT DO YOU GET WHEN YOU CROSS A
GIANT WITH A SKUNK?

A big stink!

WHAT DO YOU GET WHEN YOU CROSS
A WOLF AND AN EGG?

A very hairy omelet!

WHAT DO YOU CALL A PIG THAT WON THE LOTTERY?

Filthy rich!

WHICH SIDE OF A RAT HAS THE MOST HAIR?
The outside!

WHY DID THE ELEPHANT CROSS THE ROAD?
To pick up the squashed chicken.

WHAT DO CATS PUT IN THEIR DRINKS?
Mice cubes!

**WHO MAKES THE BEST PREHISTORIC
REPTILE CLOTHES?**
A dino-sewer!

**WHAT DID THE BANANA SAY WHEN THE ELEPHANT
STEPPED ON IT?**
Nothing...bananas don't talk!

WHY DO DINOSAURS EAT RAW MEAT?

Because they don't know how to cook!

WHAT DID THE GRAPE DO WHEN THE ELEPHANT SAT ON IT?

It gave out a little wine.

WHAT DO YOU CALL A SNAKE THAT WEARS DIAPERS?

A diaper viper.

WHAT DO YOU GET WHEN YOU CROSS A SPITZ AND A CHOW DOG?

A dog that throws up a lot.

WHAT DO YOU GIVE A PIG WITH A RASH?

Oinkment!

WHY DID THE DINOSAURS GO EXTINCT?

Because they wouldn't take a bath!

WHAT DO YOU CALL A SHEEP WITH NO LEGS?

A cloud.

WHERE DO BABY COWS GO TO EAT LUNCH?

The calf-eteria.

WHAT IS BLACK AND WHITE AND RED ALL OVER?

An exploding zebra!

WHAT IS BLACK AND WHITE AND RED ALL OVER?

A skunk with diaper rash!

HOW DID THE SKUNK CALL HOME?

On its smell phone.

WHAT DO HOUSEKEEPER RODENTS DO?

Mousework!

WHAT DID THE FARMER USE TO KEEP TRACK OF HIS COWS?

A cow-culator.

WHAT DO YOU CALL A PIG THAT LIKES TO TELL LONG, DULL STORIES?

A boar.

WHAT HAPPENS WHEN YOU PUT SNAKES ON A CAR WINDOW?

You get windshield vipers.

WHAT DO YOU GET WHEN YOU CROSS A CAT AND A PORCUPINE?

An animal that goes, "meowch" whenever it licks itself.

WHAT DO WHALES LIKE TO CHEW?

Blubber gum.

WHERE DO ALL TURKEYS GO WHEN THEY DIE?

To oven.

WHAT DO YOU GET WHEN YOU CROSS A PIG AND A CENTIPEDE?

Bacon and legs.

WHAT GOES "OOOO, OOOOOO, OOOOO?"

A cow with no lips.

WHAT IS BLACK AND WHITE, BLACK AND WHITE, BLACK AND WHITE?

A zebra caught in a revolving door.

WHAT DO DOGS EAT AT THE MOVIES?

Pup-corn.

WHAT DO YOU GET WHEN YOU CROSS A HEN WITH A POODLE?

Pooched eggs.

WHY DID TIGGER LOOK IN THE TOILET?
He was looking for Pooh!

WHAT'S GOT FOUR LEGS AND AN ARM?
A happy Rottweiler.

DID YOU HEAR ABOUT THE LADY WHO HAD A HEART TRANSPLANT FROM A SHEEP?
When the doctor asked how she felt,
she said, "Not baaaaad!"

WHAT DO YOU GET WHEN YOU CROSS A TOAD AND A CROCODILE?
A croakadile.

WHAT DO YOU GET IF YOU CROSS A DAFFODIL WITH A CROCODILE?
I don't know, but I wouldn't try sniffing it!

WHAT DO YOU GET WHEN YOU CROSS
A SKUNK AND A TV SET?

Smell-o-vision.

WHAT DO YOU DO IF YOU GET STUCK IN AN
ELEPHANT'S STOMACH?

Run around until you get pooped out!

WHAT DO YOU GET WHEN YOU CROSS
A T-REX WITH A DOG?

Something that drinks out of any toilet it wants to!

HOW DO YOU PUT A GIRAFFE INTO A REFRIGERATOR?

You open the refrigerator, put in the giraffe, and close the door.

HOW DO YOU PUT AN ELEPHANT INTO A REFRIGERATOR?

You open the refrigerator, take out the giraffe, put in the elephant, and close the door.

THE LION KING IS HAVING A PARTY, ALL THE ANIMALS GO, EXCEPT ONE. WHICH ANIMAL DOES NOT GO TO THE PARTY?

The elephant. It's in the refrigerator!

THERE IS A RIVER YOU MUST CROSS, BUT IT'S FILLED WITH CROCODILES. HOW DO YOU MANAGE?

You swim across—all the crocodiles are at the party!

A REAL HOOT

Birdie, birdie in the sky
Dropped some yucky stuff in my eye,
I'm too big to whine or cry,
I'm just glad that cows don't fly!

HOW DO YOU KNOW THAT OWLS ARE SMARTER THAN CHICKENS?

Have you ever heard of Kentucky-Fried Owl?

WHAT KIND OF BIRD GULPS THE LOUDEST?
The swallow!

WHAT DO YOU CALL A WOODPECKER WITH NO BEAK?
A headbanger!

WHAT GOES PECK, PECK, PECK, BOOM?
A chicken in a mine field.

WHAT DO YOU CALL A CHICKEN THAT CROSSES THE ROAD WITHOUT LOOKING BOTH WAYS?
Dead.

WHAT KIND OF HIT DOES A CHICKEN MAKE IN BASEBALL?

A fowl ball!

WHAT SAYS "QUICK, QUICK?"

A duck with hiccups.

WHAT IS BLACK AND WHITE AND BLUE ALL OVER?

A frozen penguin!

GRODY TO THE MAX!

WHAT IS GREEN, HAS FOUR LEGS, AND TWO TRUNKS?

Two seasick tourists.

WHY DO THEY HAVE FENCES AROUND CEMETERIES?

Because everyone's dying to get in!

WHAT DID THE CHEWING GUM SAY TO THE SHOE?

I'm stuck on you!

WHAT IS RED AND GREEN ALL OVER?

A sunburned, seasick tourist!

WHAT IS BLACK AND WHITE, BLACK AND WHITE, AND GREEN?

Two skunks fighting over a pickle!

WHAT'S THE HARDEST PART ABOUT SKY DIVING?

The ground!

WHAT IS BLACK AND WHITE AND AS HARD AS A ROCK?

A Dalmatian that fell in wet cement!

WHAT'S THE DIFFERENCE BETWEEN A TV AND A NEWSPAPER?

Ever tried swatting a fly with a TV?

WHAT SHOULD YOU DO WHEN YOU'RE DYING?

Go into the kitchen and eat some Life Savers!

WHAT IS BLACK AND WHITE, BLACK AND WHITE, AND ORANGE?

Two skunks fighting over a basketball!

WHAT GOES IN THE WATER PINK AND COMES OUT BLUE?

A swimmer on a cold day!

WHAT KIND OF HAIR DO OCEANS HAVE?

Wavy!

HOW DO YOU CHANGE A PUMPKIN INTO ANOTHER VEGETABLE?

Throw it up in the air, and when it comes down, it'll be squash.

WHAT MUSICAL INSTRUMENT DO YOU FIND IN THE BATHROOM?

A tuba toothpaste.

WHERE WAS THE FIRST DONUT MADE?

In "Grease!"

WHAT DID THE HAMBURGER NAME HIS DAUGHTER?

Patty!

WHY DID THE FIREFIGHTER BRING THE DALMATION TO THE FIRE?

To locate the nearest hydrant!

WHY IS A BASEBALL GAME LIKE A PANCAKE?

Because they both depend on the batter.

WHY DID THE SHOE CRY?

It bit its tongue.

WHAT DID THE PORK CHOP SAY TO THE STEAK?

Nice to meat you!

WHAT IS BROWN, HAIRY, AND WEARS SUNGLASSES?

A coconut on summer vacation!

**WHAT DO YOU CALL BOXER SHORTS
WITH ONLY ONE LEG?**

Blunderwear!

**WHEN DID THE UNDERWEAR LIKE BEING HUNG ON A
CLOTHES LINE?**

When they started to get the hang of it!

**WHY DIDN'T THE PAIR OF UNDERWEAR
WANT TO BE PUT AWAY?**

It was afraid that might hamper its style!

WHAT DO YOU CALL WORKING OUT IN YOUR UNDERWEAR?

Boxer-cizing.

WHAT DO YOU GET WHEN YOU PUT UNDERWEAR ON A TV SET?

A smelly telly!

WHAT DO YOU CALL BRIGHT COLORED UNDERWEAR?

Your fundies!

WHAT DO YOU CALL UNATTRACTIVE UNDERWEAR THAT ARE TOO SMALL?

Ugly snugglies!

WHAT DO YOU CALL SOMEONE WHO STEALS YOUR FAVORITE LONG UNDERWEAR?

A wooly bully!

WHAT DID THE UNDERWEAR SAY TO THE BOY?

Don't wear me out!

HOW DO YOU TELL SOMEONE THAT HE NEEDS NEW UNDERWEAR?

Briefly!

KNOCK, KNOCK.

Who's there?

ENID.

Enid who?

ENID A CLEAN PAIR OF UNDERWEAR!

KNOCK, KNOCK.

Who's there?

SABRINA.

Sabrina who?

SABRINA LONG TIME SINCE I'VE CHANGED MY UNDERWEAR!

WHAT DO YOU SAY TO PEOPLE WHO WON'T STOP TELLING UNDERWEAR JOKES?

You tell them to make it short!

DEFINITION OF A SKELETON:

A bunch of bones with the person scraped off.

DEFINITION OF AN ADULT:

A person who has stopped growing at both ends and is now growing in the middle.

DEFINITION OF DUST:

Mud with the juice squeezed out.

DEFINITION OF A CHICKEN:

An animal that can be eaten before it's born and after it's dead.

DEFINITION OF A CANNIBAL:

Someone who is fed up with people.

HOW DO LOCOMOTIVES HEAR?

With their engineers.

WHAT DO YOU GET WHEN YOU CROSS POISON IVY WITH A 4-LEAF CLOVER?

A rash of good luck.

HOW IS AN OLD COMB LIKE A HOCKEY PLAYER?

They're both missing a few teeth.

WHAT DO YOU CALL A SMELLY FAIRY?

Stinkerbell!

WHAT KIND OF JOKES DO FOOT DOCTORS LIKE?

Corny ones.

WHAT DO PLUMBERS EAT FOR BREAKFAST?

Wrench toast.

**WHAT'S LONG AND ORANGE AND
FLIES AT THE SPEED OF SOUND?**

A jet-propelled carrot.

**HOW DO KIDS WHO ARE TAKING
TESTS LIKE THEIR EGGS?**

Over easy.

67

WHAT IS A FRESH VEGETABLE?

One that insults the farmer.

WHAT HAPPENED TO THE BUTCHER WHO BACKED INTO THE MEAT GRINDER?

He got a little behind in his work.

WHAT GAMES DO COWS LIKE TO PLAY?

Moo-sical chairs.

AN APPLE A DAY KEEPS THE DOCTOR AWAY, SO WHAT DOES A JAR OF ONIONS DO?

It keeps everyone away!

WHY ARE INFORMANTS MESSY?

They're always spilling the beans!

WHY DID THE STUDENT START A FOOD FIGHT WITH HIS MEAT LOAF?

The only other option was to eat it!

WHY IS THE COOK SO FUNNY AT THE CAFETERIA?

Because she'll have your stomach in knots.

WHAT DO YOU CALL A SCHOOL CAFETERIA COOK?

The torture king!

WHY DID THE STUDENT REFUSE TO EAT HIS MYSTERY MEAT?

He wanted to have teeth left for dessert.

WHAT DO YOU CALL SOMEONE WHO LOVES EATING AT THE SCHOOL CAFETERIA?

Starving!

WHEN IS IT OKAY TO EAT AT THE SCHOOL CAFETERIA?

When it's your last meal.

WHY SHOULD YOU FINISH YOUR PLATE WHEN YOU EAT CAFETERIA FOOD?

So it won't end up on someone else's plate tomorrow!

WAITER, THERE'S A DEAD FLY IN MY SOUP.

What do you expect for a dollar? A live one?

WAITER, THERE'S A BIRD IN MY SOUP.

That's all right, madam. It's bird's nest soup.

WAITER, THERE'S A DEAD BEETLE IN MY SOUP.

Yes sir, they're not very good swimmers.

WAITER, THERE'S A FLY IN MY SOUP!

Shhh! Everyone else is going to want one!

WAITER, THIS SOUP TASTES FUNNY!

Why aren't you laughing?

WAITER, THIS COFFEE TASTES LIKE SOAP.

That must be tea, madam.
The coffee tastes like glue.

WAITER, THIS COFFEE TASTES OLD AND WEAK!

Don't complain, sir. You may be old and weak
yourself some day.

WAITER, YOUR THUMB'S IN MY SOUP!

That's all right, it's not hot.

WAITER, THERE'S A DEAD FLY IN MY SOUP!

Yes, the hot water kills them.

WAITER, YOU'RE NOT FIT TO SERVE A PIG!

I'm doing my best, madam.

WAITER, DO YOU HAVE FROG LEGS?

No, I've always walked like this.

WAITER, THERE IS A FLY IN MY SALAD.

Sorry, I didn't know that you were a vegetarian.

WAITER, THERE'S A HAIR IN MY HONEY.

It must have dropped off the comb.

WAITER, THERE'S A FLY IN MY SOUP.

No, that's a cockroach. The fly is on your toast.

**WAITER, THAT DOG'S JUST RUN OFF
WITH MY ROAST LAMB!**

Yes, it's very popular, sir.

WAITER, DO YOU SERVE CRABS?

Yes, we serve everyone.

74

WAITER, IS THERE ANY SOUP ON THE MENU?

No, I've wiped it all off.

WAITER, THIS BREAD'S GOT SAND IN IT.

That's to stop the butter from slipping off.

WAITER, THERE'S A BUTTON IN MY SOUP.

Oh, thank you, madam. I've been looking
for that everywhere.

WAITER, THERE'S A FLY ON MY STEAK.

Oh well, that's what happens with rotten meat.

WAITER, THERE'S NO CHICKEN IN THIS CHICKEN PIE.

So what? You don't get dog in a dog biscuit, do you?

WAITER, THERE'S A WORM ON MY PLATE.

That's your sausage, sir.

WAITER, THERE'S A FLY IN MY BUTTER.

No there isn't.

I TELL YOU THERE IS A FLY IN MY BUTTER!

And I tell you there isn't! It isn't a fly— it's a moth. And it isn't butter— it's margarine. So there!

WAITER, IS THIS A HAIR IN MY SOUP?

Yes, of course, it's rabbit stew!

76

HUMAN BEANS

WHAT U.S. PRESIDENT LIVED NEAR THE SEA AND ATE PEOPLE?

Jaws Washington!

WHAT DID THE SURFER THINK WHEN HE TURNED INTO A FROG?

He thought it was toad-ally awesome!

WHAT'S A GOOD LUNCH FOR SKIERS?

Ice-bergers!

IF A PLANE CRASHED ON THE SNOWY BORDERS OF NEW HAMPSHIRE AND MAINE, WHERE WOULD THEY BURY THE SURVIVORS?

Hopefully nowhere. You don't bury survivors!

77

DID YOU HEAR ABOUT THE MAN WHO WAS TAP DANCING?

He broke his ankle when he fell into the sink.

HOW MANY EARS DID DAVY CROCKETT HAVE?

Three - his left ear, his right ear, and his wild front ear.

WHY DID THE WOMAN WEAR A HELMET AT THE DINNER TABLE?

She was on a crash diet.

DID YOU HEAR ABOUT THE UNLUCKY SAILOR?

First he was shipwrecked, then he was rescued by the Titanic.

WHY WAS THE SKIER CRYING?
Because he got hit in the eye with a snowball!

WHAT DO SKIERS SING TO EACH OTHER ON BIRTHDAYS?
Freeze a jolly good fellow!

WHAT DOES THE BIKER HAVE IN HIS SHOE?
Althete's foot!

HOW DID THE BIKER FEEL AFTER CRASHING INTO A PIE SHOP?
A little crusty!

HOW DID THE STUDENT SCRAPE HIS KNEE?

On a class trip!

KNOCK, KNOCK.

Who's there?

FALAFEL.

Falafel who?

**FALAFEL MY SKATEBOARD
AND SCRAPED MY KNEE!**

WHY DID THE SKIER CRY AFTER HE HIT THE TREE?

It was a weeping willow!

**HOW DID THE FIGURE SKATER KNOW
HER SKATES WERE TIRED?**

Their tongues were hanging out!

WHAT IS BRIGHT RED AND HAS A TRUNK?

A burned surfer heading home from vacation.

WHAT DID THE GIRL SAY WHEN SHE GOT A SPLINTER IN HER HAND?

Wooden you know it!

WHAT DO YOU CALL A PIG IN A RACE CAR?

A road hog!

WHAT DOES A CANNIBAL CALL A MAN IN A HAMMOCK?

Breakfast in bed!

DID YOU HEAR ABOUT THE CANNIBAL WHO GNAWED A BONE FOR HOURS ON END?

When he stood up, he fell over.

WHAT DOES A CANNIBAL CALL A PHONE BOOK?

A menu!

WHAT HAPPENED WHEN THE CANNIBALS ATE A COMEDIAN?

They had a feast of fun!

HOW DID THE INVISIBLE BOY UPSET HIS MOTHER?

He kept appearing!

HAVE YOU EVER SEEN A MAN-EATING TIGER?

No, but in the restaurant next door,
I saw a man eating chicken.

**WHAT HAPPENED AT THE CANNIBAL'S
WEDDING PARTY?**

They toasted the bride and groom!

WHAT DO CANNIBALS CALL A HEARSE?

Meals on wheels.

WHAT DID THE CANNIBAL SAY TO THE WAITER?

I'll have a large manwich and a tossed Sally on the side.

TWO CANNIBALS WERE EATING A CLOWN. ONE SAID TO THE OTHER, "DOES THIS TASTE FUNNY TO YOU?"

WHAT DID THE CANNIBAL GET WHEN HE WAS LATE FOR DINNER?
The cold shoulder.

WHY DID THE CANNIBAL KIDNAP THE TOURIST?
He wanted takeout food.

A CANNIBAL IS A SOMEONE WHO GOES INTO A RESTAURANT AND ORDERS THE WAITER.

DID YOU HEAR ABOUT THE CANNIBAL STUDENT WHO WAS SUSPENDED FROM SCHOOL FOR BUTTERING UP THE TEACHER?

HAVE YOU HEARD ABOUT THE CANNIBAL RESTAURANT WHERE DINNER COSTS AN ARM AND A LEG?

WHAT'S A CANNIBAL'S FAVORITE SOUP?
One with a lot of body.

TWO CANNIBALS WERE EATING DINNER. ONE SAID, "I REALLY DON'T LIKE MY TEACHER."
The other said, "Well, just eat the noodles."

TWO FEROCIOUS CANNIBALS SAT LICKING THEIR FINGERS AFTER A LARGE MEAL. "YOUR FRIEND MAKES A DELICIOUS ROAST," ONE SAID.

"Thanks," his friend said, "I'm gonna miss her!"

A CANNIBAL VISITED HIS NEIGHBOR TO ADMIRE HIS NEW REFRIGERATOR.
"HOW MUCH CAN IT HOLD?" THE MAN ASKED.

"I'm not sure," the neighbor said. "But it holds the two men that brought it."

WHAT DO CANNIBALS EAT FOR DESSERT?

Chocolate covered aunts.

WHY DON'T CANNIBALS EAT WEATHER FORECASTERS?

Because they give them wind.

WHAT IS A CANNIBAL'S FAVORITE TYPE OF TV SHOW?
A celebrity roast.

**THE FIRST CANNIBAL ASKED THE 2ND CANNIBAL,
"AREN'T YOU DONE EATING YET?"**
The 2nd cannibal replied, "I'm on my last leg now."

**DID YOU HEAR ABOUT THE CANNIBAL WHO
LOVED FAST FOOD?**
He ordered a pizza with everybody on it.

**WHAT'S THE DIFFERENCE BETWEEN
A DENTIST AND A YANKEES FAN?**
One roots for the Yanks and the other
yanks for the roots!

WHAT'S A DENTIST'S FAVORITE RIDE?

The molar coaster.

WHY DID THE MOSQUITO GO TO THE DENTIST?

To improve his bite.

WHAT DO YOU GET IF YOU CROSS
A DENTIST WITH A WEASEL?

The Tooth Ferret.

WHAT IS BEETHOVEN DOING IN HIS GRAVE?

De-composing!

WHY COULDN'T BATMAN GO FISHING?
Robin ate all the worms!

WHAT DO YOU CALL A GUY WHO'S BORN IN COLUMBUS, GROWS UP IN CLEVELAND, AND THEN DIES IN CINCINNATI?
Dead.

MOMMY, WHAT HAPPENED TO ALL THAT DOG FOOD FIDO WOULDN'T EAT?
Just eat your meat loaf!

WHAT DO YOU CALL A FLYING POLICEMAN?
A heli-copper.

89

WHAT KIND OF DESSERT DOES A MATH TEACHER BAKE?

Pi.

DID YOU HEAR ABOUT THE LADY THAT WALKED THROUGH A SCREEN DOOR?

She strained herself.

WHY WAS THE POLICE OFFICER SMELLY?

Because he was on duty.

IF ATHLETES GET ATHLETES FOOT, WHAT DO ASTRONAUTS GET?

Missle-toe.

WHAT DO YOU GET WHEN MORONS HAVE BABIES?

More-ons.

MOMMY, WHAT'S A VAMPIRE?

Drink your juice before it clots!

MOMMY, I DON'T WANT TO GO TO AUSTRALIA.

Just keep swimming!

MONSTER MADNESS

WHAT WEREWOLF CAME TO VISIT CINDERELLA?

Her hairy godmother.

WHAT DO MONSTERS MAKE WITH CARS?

Traffic jam.

WHAT DOES GODZILLA DRIVE?

A monster truck!

WHAT DO YOU GET IF YOU CROSS A MONSTER WITH A GOAT?

A dirty kid that scares people away.

WHY DID THE MONSTER REMOVE HIS NOSE?

To see what made it run.

MONSTER 1: Am I late for dinner?

MONSTER 2: Yes, everyone has been eaten.

WHY DID THE MONSTER EAT THE NORTH POLE?

He was in the mood for a frozen dinner!

DID YOU HEAR ABOUT THE VAIN MONSTER WHO WAS GOING BALD?

The doctor couldn't do a hair transplant for him, so he shrunk his head to fit his hair.

WHAT GOES HA HA HA PLUNK?

A monster laughing his head off.

WHY ARE DRAGONS BAD BOSSES?

Because they keep firing people.

WHY DID THE MONSTER GO INTO HOSPITAL?

To have his ghoul-stones removed.

WHAT KIND OF MONSTER IS HAPPIEST SITTING AT THE END OF YOUR FINGER?

The boogie man!

WHAT IS A MONSTERS BEST DAY OF THE WEEK?
Chewsday.

WHAT KIND OF FUR DO YOU GET FROM A WEREWOLF?
As fur away as you can get!

WHAT DO YOU CALL A SWAMP MONSTER THAT EATS UP ALL THE WILDLIFE?
A toad-hog!

IGOR: How was that science fiction movie you saw last night?
DR. FRANKENSTEIN: Oh, the same old story - boy meets girl, boy loses girl, boy builds new girl!

BOY MONSTER: You've got a face like a million dollars!
GIRL MONSTER: Really?
BOY MONSTER: Yes - it's green and wrinkly!

WHAT IS A SWAMP MONSTER'S FAVORITE FLOWER?
The croak-us!

WHAT DO YOU FIND IN A MONSTER'S BELLY BUTTON?
A gob-lint!

WHAT DO YOU CALL A HAIRY MONSTER
IN BOXER SHORTS?
An under-were-wolf!

WHAT DID THE RODENT SAY TO THE MONSTER?

Mice to meet you!

WHAT DO THE FANS SAY TO CYCLOPS WHEN HE'S UP AT BAT?

Keep your eye on the ball!

WHAT DID GODZILLA HAVE AT THE "ALL YOU CAN EAT" RESTAURANT?

The waiters!

WHAT IS A SEA MONSTER'S FAVORITE DISH?

Fish and ships.

WHAT DO THEY HAVE FOR LUNCH AT MONSTER SCHOOL?

Human beans, boiled legs, pickled bunions,
and eye-scream.

WHY DID THE MONSTER PUT A BANANA PEEL IN FRONT OF THE CLOSET?

So he could slip into something more comfortable.

WHAT DID BIGFOOT GROW IN HIS GARDEN?

Sas-squash!

WHERE DO YOU FIND A MONSTER WITH ONLY ONE HAND?

In a second-hand store!

WHERE DO SLIMY MONSTERS SHOP?

At the gross-ery store.

WHAT DO YOU DO WITH A GREEN MONSTER?

Put him in the sun until he ripens.

HOW DO YOU KNOW IF A MONSTER HAS COME AROUND FOR LUNCH?

There are muddy footprints on the carpet.

WHAT WATERY CREATURE NEVER LEARNS TO TELL TIME?

The Clock-Less Monster.

HOW DOES A MONSTER LIKE ITS EGGS?

Terri-fried.

WHY DID BIGFOOT MONSTER WALK THROUGH THE MUD?

He wanted to make a big impression.

WHAT DO YOU CALL A MONSTER THAT NEVER KNOCKS?

The Knock Less Monster.

WHAT'S A LITTLE MONSTER'S FAVORITE GAME?

Hide and shriek.

WHAT DOES A MONSTER READ IN A MAGAZINE?
Her horror-scope.

WHERE DO MONSTERS GO ON VACATION?
Death Valley.

WHY DID THE MONSTER HAVE TWINS IN HIS LUNCH BOX?
Just in case he wanted seconds.

MONSTER: How much are those kittens in the window?
CLERK: They're $12 a piece.
MONSTER: Okay, I'll have a piece of the black one and a piece of the orange one.

101

CREEPY CRAWLY CRACKUPS

WHY DID THE SPIDER TAKE A LAPTOP TO THE BEACH?
So it could surf the web.

**WHAT DID THE MOSQUITO SAY THE FIRST
TIME IT SAW A CAMEL?**
Did I do that?

WHERE DO HORNETS GO WHEN THEY'RE SICK?
To the waspital.

WHAT IS A MOSQUITO'S FAVORITE SPORT?
Skin diving!

WHAT DO YOU CALL A FLY WITHOUT WINGS?
A walk.

WHY ARE SPIDERS GOOD AT BASEBALL?
They know how to catch flies.

WHERE DOES A SPIDER CHECK ITS SPELLING?
In Webster's.

WHY WAS THE FATHER CENTIPEDE SO UPSET?
All of the kids needed new shoes!

WHY DID THE SNAIL PAINT AN "S" ON ITS CAR?

So people would say "Look at that S car go!"

HOW DO YOU MAKE A SLUG DRINK?

Stick it in the blender.

WHAT'S ANOTHER NAME FOR A SNAIL?

A booger with a crash helmet.

WHAT DO YOU CALL A SNAIL ON A BOAT?

A snailer.

WHY WAS THE SPY SO AFRAID OF INSECTS?
Because he knew he was being bugged!

WHAT DID ONE SILK SPINNER SAY TO THE OTHER?
Don't try to worm your way out of this!

I AM FOUND IN THE SEA AND ON LAND, BUT I DO NOT WALK OR SWIM. I TRAVEL BY FOOT, BUT I AM TOE-LESS. I'M NEVER FAR FROM HOME. WHAT AM I?
Answer: A snail

WHAT GOES HUM-CHOO, HUM CHOO?
A bee with a cold!

WHAT DO YOU CALL AN INSECT SPY?

Insect-or Gadget!

**WHAT LIES ON ITS BACK, 100 FEET
IN THE AIR?**

A dead centipede.

**WHAT DO YOU GET WHEN YOU CROSS A VAMPIRE
WITH A MOSQUITO?**

A very itchy neck!

**WHAT DO YOU GET WHEN YOU CROSS BATMAN &
ROBIN WITH A STEAMROLLER?**

Flatman & Ribbon!

WHAT KIND OF INSECT LIVES IN SOME UNDERWEAR?
The button fly!

WHY DID THE SPY GO TO WORK DRESSED AS A BEE?
Because it knew there was going to be a sting!

WHAT DOES A BEE SAY BEFORE IT STINGS YOU?
This is going to hurt me a lot more than it hurts you!

**WHAT'S MORE DANGEROUS THAN
BEING WITH A FOOL?**
Fooling with a bee!

WHAT DO YOU GET IF YOU CROSS A BEE WITH A SKUNK?

An animal that stinks and stings!

WHAT DOES A QUEEN BEE DO WHEN SHE BURPS?

She issues a royal pardon!

WHAT DID ONE BEE SAY TO THE OTHER BEE IN SUMMER?

Swarm out here, isn't it?

WHY DO BEES HAVE STICKY HAIR?

Because of the honey combs!

**WHAT FLIES AROUND YOUR LIGHT AT NIGHT
AND CAN BITE OFF YOUR HEAD?**
A tiger moth!

WHAT IS THE DEFINITION OF A CATERPILLAR?
A worm in a fur coat!

**WHY DID THE DETECTIVE THINK THE SPY
WAS AN INSECT?**
Because he was a fly-by-night!

WHAT DO YOU DO IF YOU HAVE BUGS IN YOUR BED?
Kill one and the rest will go to the funeral!

WHAT DID ONE CENTIPEDE SAY TO THE OTHER CENTIPEDE?

You've got a lovely pair of legs, You've got a lovely pair of legs, you've got a lovely pair of legs, you've got a lovely pair of legs, you've got a lovely pair of legs...!

WHAT IS WORSE THAN AN ALLIGATOR WITH A TOOTHACHE?

A centipede with athlete's foot!

WHAT GOES 99-CLONK, 99-CLONK, 99-CLONK?

A centipede with a wooden leg!

WHAT DO TWO TERMITES SAY WHEN THEY SEE A HOUSE ON FIRE?

Barbecue tonight?

HOW DO WE KNOW THAT INSECTS ARE SMART?
They always know when you're eating outside!

WHAT HAS SIX LEGS, BITES, AND TALKS IN CODE?
A Morse-quito!

WHAT IS THE DIFFERENCE BETWEEN A MOSQUITO AND A FLY?
Try zipping up a mosquito!

WHAT HAS ANTLERS AND SUCKS BLOOD?
A moose-quito!

WHAT HAS 245 PAIRS OF SNEAKERS, A BALL, AND TWO HOOPS?

A centipede basketball team.

WHY ARE MOSQUITOS RELIGIOUS?

They prey on you!

HOW DO YOU MAKE A BUTTERFLY?

Throw butter.

WHAT DO YOU CALL A WORM IN A APPLE?

A teacher's pet.

WHAT'S THE BIGGEST MOTH IN THE WORLD?
A mammoth!

WHY DID THE MOTH NIBBLE A HOLE IN THE CARPET?
He wanted to see the floor show!

WHY WAS THE MOTH SO UNPOPULAR?
He kept picking holes in everything!

WHAT DO YOU GET IF YOU CROSS
A FIREFLY AND A MOTH?
An insect that can find its way around a dark closet.

WHAT DO YOU CALL A GRASSHOPPER WITH NO LEGS?

A grasshover!

HOW CAN YOU TELL WHICH END OF A WORM IS WHICH?

Tickle it in the middle and see which end laughs!

WHAT DID THE SLUG SAY TO THE OTHER WHO HAD HIT HIM AND RUN OFF?

I'll get you next slime!

WHAT DO YOU CALL A QUIET BEE?

A mumble-bee.

WHAT IS THE DEFINITION OF A SLUG?
A snail with a housing problem!

**WHAT DID THE SLUG SAY AS HE SLIPPED
DOWN THE WALL?**
How slime flies!

HOW DO YOU KNOW YOUR KITCHEN FLOOR IS DIRTY?
The slugs leave a trail on the floor that says, "Wash me!"

WHAT DO YOU DO WHEN TWO SNAILS HAVE A FIGHT?
Leave them to slug it out!

WHERE DO YOU FIND GIANT SNAILS?
At the end of giants fingers!

WHAT DOES A SPIDER DO WHEN IT GETS ANGRY?
It goes up the wall!

WHAT WOULD HAPPEN IF TARANTULAS WERE AS BIG AS HORSES?
If you got bit by one, you could ride it to hospital!

WHAT DO YOU GET IF YOU CROSS A SPIDER AND AN ELEPHANT?
I'm not sure, but if you see one walking across the ceiling, run before it collapses!

WHAT DID THE SPIDER SAY TO THE FLY?

We're getting married, do you
want to come to the webbing?

WHAT HAPPENED WHEN THE CHEF FOUND A DADDY LONG LEGS IN THE SALAD?

It became a daddy short legs!

WHAT DO YOU GET IF YOU CROSS A TARANTULA WITH A ROSE?

I'm not sure, but I wouldn't try smelling it!

WHAT IS RED AND DANGEROUS?

Strawberry and tarantula jelly!

117

WHAT'S THE HEALTHIEST INSECT?

A vitamin bee.

WHAT HAPPENED TO THE BEE THAT FELL IN LOVE?

It got stuck on its honey.

WHY DON'T BABY BIRDS SMILE?

Would you smile if your mother fed you worms all day?

WHAT HAS 50 LEGS AND CAN'T WALK?

Half a centipede.

WHAT'S YELLOW, WIGGLES, AND IS DANGEROUS?

A maggot with attitude!

WHAT DO WORMS LEAVE ROUND THEIR BATHS?

The scum of the earth!

**WHAT DO YOU GET IF YOU CROSS
A WORM AND AN ELEPHANT?**

Very big worm holes in your garden!

WHAT READS AND LIVES IN AN APPLE?

A bookworm!

WHAT DID THE WOODWORM SAY TO THE CHAIR?

It's been nice gnawing you!

WHAT DO YOU GET IF YOU CROSS
A WORM AND A YOUNG GOAT?

A dirty kid!

WHAT DO YOU GET IF YOU CROSS
A GLOW WORM WITH A PYTHON?

A 15 foot strip of light that can strangle you to death!

WHAT IS THE BEST ADVICE TO GIVE TO A WORM?

Sleep late!

WHAT'S THE DIFFERENCE BETWEEN A WORM AND AN APPLE?

Have you ever tried worm pie?

WHAT IS THE LAST THING TO GO THROUGH A BUG'S MIND BEFORE HE HITS THE WINDSHIELD?

His backside!

WHY DO WORMS TASTE LIKE CHEWING GUM?

Because they're wrigleys.

WHAT DO BEES DO WITH THEIR HONEY?

They cell it.

WHAT IS WORSE THAN FINDING A WORM IN YOUR APPLE?

Finding half a worm in your apple!

WHAT DID THE MAGGOT SAY TO HIS FRIEND WHEN HE GOT STUCK IN AN APPLE?

Worm your way out of that one.

WHAT HAPPENED TO THE GLOW WORM WHO WAS SQUASHED?

He was de-lighted.

WHAT GOES "SNAP, CRACKLE, AND POP?"

A firefly with a short circuit!

WHICH FLY MAKES FILMS?
Stephen Speilbug!

WHY DID THE FLY FLY?
Because the spider spied her.

WHAT IS THE DIFFERENCE BETWEEN A FLEA-BITTEN DOG AND A BORED VISITOR?
One's going to itch, and the other is itching to go!

HOW TO FLEAS TRAVEL?
Itch hiking!

WHAT IS THE MOST FAITHFUL INSECT?

A flea, once they find someone they like,
they stick to them!

WHAT IS THE DIFFERENCE BETWEEN
A FLEA AND A WOLF?

One prowls on the hairy, and the other howls
on the prairie!

A REAL SCREAM!

WHY DO GHOSTS GO TO BASEBALL GAMES?
To boo the umpires.

WHAT'S A GHOST'S FAVORITE BASEBALL TEAM?
The Toronto Boo Jays.

WHEN DO GHOSTS USUALLY APPEAR?
Just before someone screams.

WHAT DO GHOSTS SPREAD ON BAGELS?
Scream cheese!

WHAT ROOM DIDN'T THE GHOST DARE TO GO INTO?

The living room!

WHAT IS A SPOOK'S FAVORITE RIDE?

A roller-ghoster!

DID YOU HEAR ABOUT THE DUMB GHOST?

He climbed over the wall.

WHAT'S A GHOST'S FAVORITE MAGAZINE?

Good House-Creeping.

**WHAT DO YOU GET WHEN YOU MIX
A COW AND A GHOST?**

Vanishing cream!

WHAT KIND OF PASTA DO GHOSTS EAT?

Spook-ghetti!

**HOW DOES A GHOST FEEL AFTER
HEARING CREEPY MUSIC?**

Ear-ee!

WHY CAN'T THE INVISIBLE BOY PASS SCHOOL?

The teacher always marks him absent!

WHY DIDN'T THE GHOST EAT LIVER?

He didn't have the stomach for it!

WHAT DOES A GHOST MISS MOST WHEN IT MOVES OUT OF TOWN?

All of its possessions.

WHAT DO YOU CALL A DEAD CHICKEN THAT LIKES TO SCARE PEOPLE?

A poultry-geist.

WHAT DO YOU CALL BIRDS THAT HAUNT YOUR BACK YARD?

Polter-geese.

WHAT DO GHOSTS LIKE ON THEIR TURKEY?

Grave-y!

WHAT DO YOU CALL GHOSTS THAT FLY OVER THE BAY?

Sea-ghouls!

WHAT IS A GHOST'S FAVORITE BED TIME STORY?

Little Boo Peep!

WHAT DO YOU FIND UP A GHOST'S NOSE?

Boo-gers!

KNOCK, KNOCK.
Who's there?
GHOST.
Ghost who?
GHOST TO SHOW YOU, NOBODY REMEMBERS MY NAME!

WHY CAN'T GHOSTS SING IN CHURCH?
Because they don't have organs!

WHAT DO YOU SAY WHEN YOU MEET A GHOST?
How do you boo?

WHY IS A GHOST A PHONY?
You can see right through him!

WHAT DID THE GHOST SAY TO HIS VISITORS IN THE HOSPITAL?

Well, do you want to hear about my apparition?

WHY DO DEVILS AND GHOSTS GET ALONG SO WELL?

Because demons are a ghoul's best friend!

WHAT DO YOU CALL A GHOST'S MOTHER AND FATHER?

Transparents.

HOW MANY DEAD PEOPLE ARE THERE IN A GRAVEYARD?

All of 'em!

WHAT'S A GOOD GIFT FOR A BABY GHOST?

Boo-ties.

WHAT DOES A LITTLE GHOST LIKE IN THE BATHTUB?

Lots of boo-bles!

WHAT DOES A GHOST DO WHEN HE GETS IN A CAR?

Puts his sheet belt on!

WHAT DO LITTLE GHOSTS CHEW?

Boo-ble gum.

WHY WOULDN'T THE GHOST STAY IN THE HAUNTED HOUSE?

He was just passing through.

WHERE DOES A BABY GHOST SIT?

In a boo-ster seat.

WHAT KIND OF MISTAKE DOES A GHOST MAKE?

A boo-boo!

WHAT DO YOU CALL A GHOST THAT BRAGS?

A ghost boaster.

WHAT DO YOU GIVE A TEENAGE GHOST FOR A GIFT?

A booooom box.

WHAT KIND OF BOOKS DO GHOSTS LIKE TO READ?

Boo-it-yourself books.

WHAT DO YOU CALL A GHOST WITH A BELL?

A dead ringer.

WHAT DO YOU GET IF YOU CROSS A GHOST AND A DOG?

A haunting dog.

**WHAT DO YOU GET WHEN A GHOST GETS
TOO CLOSE TO A CAMPFIRE?**

A ghost roast.

WHAT IS A GHOST'S FAVORITE DAY OF THE WEEK?

Moan-day.

WHAT DO YOU CALL A GHOST WITH A BELL?

A dead ringer.

WHY IS A HAUNTED HANDKERCHIEF SO SCARY?

Because it has boo-gers!

**WHAT DO YOU CALL A GHOST THAT
LIVES IN CALIFORNIA?**

A coast ghost.

WHAT DO YOU CALL A HOUSE-CLEANING GHOST?

A ghost duster.

**WHAT DO YOU CALL A GHOST WHO
POPS ALL THE BALLOONS?**

A ghost buster.

WHY ARE GRAVEYARDS SO NOISY?

Because of all the coffin.

WHAT DOES A MOTHER GHOST SAY TO HER SON?
Don't spook until you're spooken to.

WHEN CAN'T YOU BURY PEOPLE WHO LIVE OPPOSITE A GRAVEYARD?
When they're not dead.

HOW DOES A GHOUL FIND A FRIEND IN A CEMETERY?
He sees what he can dig up.

WHAT DID THE GHOUL-FRIEND SAY WHEN THE GHOUL ASKED HER TO MARRY HIM?
Of corpse I will!

WHAT'S A GHOUL'S FAVORITE DRINK?

Ghoul-ade.

WHAT KIND OF JEWELS DO GHOULS WEAR?

Tombstones.

WHAT DO YOU GET IF YOU CROSSED A GHOUL WITH A COW?

Ghost beef.

HOW IS A GHOUL LIKE AN APPLE?

Both are rotten to the core.

FANG-TASTICALLY FUNNY!

WHAT HAPPENED AT THE VAMPIRE OLYMPICS?

All the races finished neck and neck.

WHAT IS A VAMPIRE'S FAVORITE ICE CREAM?

Veinilla.

WHAT HAPPENED TO THE MAD VAMPIRE?

He went a little batty.

WHAT'S A VAMPIRE'S FAVORITE ANIMAL?

Giraffe.

IN WHAT DO VAMPIRES CROSS THE SEA?

Blood vessels.

WHY DON'T VAMPS LIKE THE RED CROSS?

They can't stand the competition.

WHY DON'T VAMPIRES LIKE MOSQUITOS?

Even more competition!

WHY DO VAMPIRES CHEW GUM?

They don't want to have bat breath.

WHAT DO VAMPIRES WEAR IN THE FALL?

Their bat-to-school clothes!

WHAT ARE A VAMPIRE'S FAVORITE FRUITS?

Adam's apples and neck-tarines.

WHAT DID THE BAT SAY TO HIS VALENTINE?

I love hanging around you.

WHAT IS A VAMPIRE'S FAVORITE KIND OF COFFEE?

De-coffin-ated!

WHERE DID THEY PUT DRACULA WHEN HE WAS ARRESTED?

In a red blood cell.

WHAT DO YOU GET IF YOU CROSS A VAMPIRE AND A COW?

A hamburger that bites back.

WHERE DOES DRACULA LIKE TO WATERSKI?

Lake Eerie.

DID YOU HEAR ABOUT THE NEW DRACULA DOLL?

Wind it up and it bites Barbie on the neck.

WHY DO VAMPIRES MAKE GREAT ARTISTS?

They have a lot of practice drawing blood.

WHY IS THERE NO STORY ABOUT A VAMPIRE WITH A BROKEN TOOTH?

There's just no point to it.

WHAT DID DRACULA SAY WHEN HE KISSED HIS VAMPIRE GIRLFRIEND?

Ouch.

WHAT DO YOU GET WHEN YOU CROSS A WEREWOLF AND A VAMPIRE?

A fur coat that fangs around your neck.

WHAT DO YOU GET IF YOU CROSS A VAMPIRE WITH A FLEA?

A lot of worried dogs.

WHAT DO YOU GET WHEN YOU CROSS A GHOST WITH AN OWL?

Something that scares people and doesn't give a hoot.

WHY WON'T ANYONE KISS DRACULA?

He has bat breath!

WHAT SPORT DOES DRACULA PLAY?

Casket-ball.

WHY DID THE VAMPIRE BABY STOP EATING BABY FOOD?

He wanted something to get his teeth into.

WACKY WIZARDS AND WITCHES

WHAT HAPPENED TO THE WITCH WHO WAS CAUGHT CHEATING?

She was ex-spelled.

WHAT DID THE WIZARD SAY TO THE LAZY MONSTER?

Quit dragon your tail!

WHY DO WITCHES FLY ON BROOM STICKS?

Because it's better than walking!

HOW DO YOU MAKE A WITCH SCRATCH?

Take away the W!

HOW DID THE WITCH KNOW IT WAS EXACTLY TWELVE NOON?

She used her witch watch!

WHY WAS THE WITCH LATE?

Her broom over swept!

WHAT'S A WITCH'S FAVORITE DOG?

A terror-eer!

WHY DON'T WITCHES LIKE TO RIDE THEIR BROOMS WHEN THEY'RE ANGRY?

They're afraid they'll fly off the handle.

WHAT IS A WITCH'S FAVORITE PET?

A wart hog!

HOW DO WITCHES KEEP THEIR HAIR IN PLACE?

They use scare spray!

HOW MUCH DOES A WITCH'S SPELL COST?

A charm and a leg!

WHAT DID THE WITCH GET WHEN SHE STUCK HER NOSE INSIDE A JAR?

Ring around the nosie!

HOW DOES A WIZARD GET RID OF TERMITES?

He has them hex-terminated.

WHY DO WIZARDS LOVE TO EAT AT BUFFET-STYLE RESTAURANTS?

Because they have the biggest potions!

WHAT'S EVIL AND UGLY ON THE INSIDE AND GREEN ON THE OUTSIDE?

A witch dressed as a cucumber.

WHAT DO WIZARDS CALL PHONY SPELLS?

Hocus bogus!

HOW DO WITCHES ROAST THEIR MARSHMALLOWS?

With dragon breath!

WHY COULDN'T THE WITCH FLY?

She was broom-sick!

WHAT IS THE MOST POWERFUL KIND OF WITCH'S BROOM?

The one that has 300 hearse-power.

WHY DO WITCHES FLY TO THEIR SECRET CAVES?
Because it's too far to walk!

WHY DON'T WITCHES LIKE TO CAST SPELLS ON BOATS?
They get potion sickness!

WHY DID THE WIZARD WEAR RED, WHITE, AND BLUE SUSPENDERS?
To keep his pants up.

WHAT'S EVIL, UGLY, AND BOUNCES?
A witch on a trampoline.

WHAT DO THE YOUNG WITCHES CALL THEIR OLDEST TEACHER?

Tyrannosaurus Hex!

WHY DON'T SINGLE WIZARDS DANCE?

Because they don't have ghoul-friends.

WHAT DID THE WIZARD SAY TO HIS GIRLFRIEND?

Darling, you look wand-erful!

TO WHAT DANCE DID THE WIZARD TAKE THE WITCH?

The Crystal Ball!

DEADLY FUNNY!

WHAT'S THE TITLE OF THE MUMMY'S NEW BOOK?

Mummies for Dummies.

WHAT DO YOU CALL A FRIENDLY MUMMY?

A chummy mummy.

**WHAT DID THE ARCHAEOLOGIST SAY
TO THE TOMB ROBBER?**

Show me the mummy!

WHAT'S A MUMMY'S FAVORITE KIND OF MUSIC?

Wrap.

WHAT DOES A MUMMY EAT FOR BREAKFAST?

Dreaded Wheat!

WHAT HAPPENED WHEN THE ICE MONSTER GOT ANGRY WITH THE ZOMBIE?

He gave him the cold shoulder.

SHOULD I TELL YOU THE STORY OF THE BODY SNATCHERS?

No, I'd better not, you might get carried away.

WHAT DID THE ZOMBIE EAT AFTER ITS TEETH WERE PULLED OUT?
The dentist.

WHY DID THE ZOMBIE GO TO HOSPITAL?
He wanted to learn a few sick jokes.

HOW DO YOU KNOW A ZOMBIE IS TIRED?
He's dead on his feet.

WHAT DO YOU DO WHEN 50 ZOMBIES SURROUND YOUR HOUSE?
Hope it's Halloween.

WHAT'S A ZOMBIE'S FAVORITE DOG?

A Rot-weiler!

WHY DIDN'T THE ZOMBIE LOOK FOR FOOD IN THE TRASH?

Because he thought it was a waste of time!

WHAT DID THE ZOMBIE GET A MEDAL FOR?

Deadication.

WHAT DID THE ZOMBIE SAY AFTER HIDING IN THE BUSHES?

I made a rash decision!

WHERE DO ZOMBIES GO FOR CRUISES?

The Deaditerranean Sea.

WHAT DID THE ZOMBIE'S FRIEND SAY WHEN HE INTRODUCED HIM TO HIS GIRLFRIEND?

Good grief! Where did you dig her up?

OUTTA THIS WORLD!

WHAT'S A MARTIAN'S NORMAL EYESIGHT?
20/20/20/20/20

WHAT KIND OF TICKS DO YOU FIND ON THE MOON?
Luna-ticks.

WHAT DID THE ALIEN SAY TO THE GAS PUMP?
Don't you know it's rude to stick your finger in your ear when I'm talking to you?

WHAT DO ALIENS DO AFTER THEY GET MARRIED?
They go on a honeyearth.

WHAT DO ASTRONAUTS WEAR TO KEEP WARM?
Apollo-neck sweaters.

WHERE DO ASTRONAUTS LEAVE THEIR SPACESHIP?
At parking meteors.

WHAT KIND OF MUSIC DO MARTIANS ENJOY?
Neptunes!

WHAT DID ONE SHOOTING STAR SAY TO THE OTHER?
Pleased to meteor.

HOW DO YOU GET A BABY ASTRONAUT TO SLEEP?
You rock-et.

WHAT DID THE BIG STAR SAY TO THE LITTLE STAR?
You're too young to go out at night.

WHAT DO YOU CALL A SPACE MAGICIAN?
A flying sorcerer.

FIRST SPACEMAN: I'm hungry.
SECOND SPACEMAN: So am I, it must be launch time.

WHAT DO YOU SAY TO A LOONY SPACEMAN?

And what high hopes you have!

WHAT DO YOU CALL AN OVERWEIGHT E.T.?

An extra cholesterol.

WHAT DO YOU CALL 12-DOZEN WORMS ON A SPACESHIP?

Gross!

WHAT DID THE METRIC ALIEN SAY?

Take me to your liter.

WHAT DID THE GARDEN ALIEN SAY?

Take me to your weeder.

WHAT DID THE LIBRARIAN ALIEN SAY?

Take me to your reader!

WHAT DO YOU CALL A ROBOT THAT ALWAYS TAKES THE LONGEST ROUTE AROUND?

R2 detour.

DO ANDROIDS HAVE SISTERS?

No, just transistors.

NAME A MARTIAN POP IDOL.

Ricky Martian!

RIB TICKLERS

WHY DO SKELETONS MAKE BAD LIARS?
Because you can see right through them.

WHAT'S A GOOD GIFT FOR A LITTLE SKELETON?
A dead-dy bear.

WHERE DO SKELETONS SWIM?
In the Dead Sea.

WHAT DOES A SKELETON SAY BEFORE EATING?

Bone appetit!

WHAT DO YOU SAY TO A SKELETON THAT IS GOING ON A TRIP?

Bone voyage.

WHAT DID THE SKELETON ORDER AT THE RESTAURANT?

Spare ribs.

WHAT DO YOU SAY WHEN A SKELETON ISN'T A GOOD LISTENER?

In one ear, out the other.

WHAT DO YOU GET IF YOU CROSS A SKELETON AND A GENIE?

Wishbones.

WHAT DID THE SKELETON SAY TO HER HUSBAND?

I love every bone in your body.

WHY DID THE SKELETON LOSE THE RACE?

His heart wasn't in it.

WHY WAS ONE SKELETON MAD AT THE OTHER?

Because he had a bone to pick with him.

**WHY DID THE FOOD QUICKLY DISAPPEAR
AT THE HALLOWEEN PARTY?**

Everyone was a goblin.

**WHAT DO YOU CALL AN OVERWEIGHT
JACK-O'-LANTERN?**

A plum-kin.

FUNNY FARM FACTOIDS

A CROCODILE CAN'T STICK OUT ITS TONGUE.

An elephant can be pregnant for up to two years.

A LION'S ROAR CAN BE HEARD UP TO FIVE MILES AWAY.

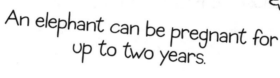

A giraffe's heart weighs about 25 pounds.

THE AFRICAN ELEPHANT'S EARS WEIGH MORE THAN 100 POUNDS EACH.

Elephants have been known to remain standing after they die.

THE ELEPHANT IS THE ONLY ANIMAL WITH FOUR KNEES.

A mole can dig a tunnel 300 feet long in one night.

A shark will die if it touches the bottom of the ocean.

A FOUR-FOOT CHILD CAN FIT INSIDE A HIPPO'S WIDE-OPEN MOUTH.

Elephants are the only animals that can't jump.

A COCKROACH CAN LIVE SEVERAL WEEKS WITH ITS HEAD CUT OFF!

SLUGS HAVE FOUR NOSES.

Some ribbon worms will eat themselves if they can't find any food.

OVER 1,000 BIRDS A YEAR DIE FROM SMASHING INTO WINDOWS!

A goldfish has an attention span of three seconds.

Animals that lay eggs don't have belly buttons.

BEAVERS CAN HOLD THEIR BREATH FOR 45 MINUTES.

A bee has five eyes.

GIRAFFES HAVE NO VOCAL CORDS.

NO TWO LIONS HAVE THE SAME PATTERN OF WHISKERS.

Flamingos turn pink from eating shrimp.

FROGS SWALLOW WITH THEIR EYES CLOSED.

Cats have more than 100 vocal cords.

173

A hummingbird weighs less then a penny.

SHRIMP CAN ONLY SWIM BACKWARD.

Fish cough.

A CATFISH HAS MORE THAN 27,000 TASTE BUDS.

A FLEA CAN JUMP 350 TIMES ITS BODY LENGTH.

Snakes can see through their eyelids.

BUTTERFLIES TASTE WITH THEIR FEET.

Armadillos can be house-trained.

175

Bats can eat 3000 mosquitoes in one night

AN OSTRICH'S EYE IS BIGGER THAN ITS BRAIN.

A jellyfish is 95 percent water.

STARFISH DON'T HAVE BRAINS.

A PREGNANT GOLDFISH IS CALLED A "TWIT."

Rabbits and guinea pigs don't sweat.

RATS AND HORSES CAN'T VOMIT.

Koalas get fluids from eucalyptus leaves, so they don't drink water.

The female lion does more than 90 percent of the hunting while the male prefers to rest.

PORCUPINES FLOAT IN WATER.

Camels have three eyelids.

PINK DOLPHINS LIVE IN THE AMAZON RIVER.

DOLPHINS CAN SWIM AND SLEEP AT THE SAME TIME.

A dolphin can kill a shark by ramming it with its snout.

DENMARK HAS MORE PIGS THAN HUMANS.

Deer cannot eat hay.

Rabbits can suffer from heat stroke.

BEAVERS CAN HOLD THEIR BREATH FOR 45 MINUTES.

 Giraffes are unable to cough.

SHARKS CAN SENSE A DROP OF BLOOD FROM 2.5 MILES (4 KM) AWAY.

Sharks can survive for six weeks without eating.

SHARKS CAN LIVE UP TO 100 YEARS.

A shark is the only fish that can blink with both eyes.

A shark's skeleton is made up of cartilage.

MOST BULLETS CANNOT PENETRATE A HIPPO'S THICK SKIN.

A pig always sleeps on its right side.

THE GIANT SQUID HAS THE LARGEST EYES IN THE WORLD.

182

SNAKES DON'T BITE IN RIVERS OR SWAMPS BECAUSE THEY WOULD DROWN IF THEY DID.

The African Rock Python can survive for two years without eating.

SPOTTED SKUNKS DO HANDSTANDS BEFORE THEY SPRAY.

A human can detect a skunk's spray a mile away.

DARK COMEDY!

DID YOU HEAR ABOUT THE GIRL WHO FOLLOWED ROAD SAFETY BY WEARING WHITE AT NIGHT?

Last winter she was knocked down by a snow plow.

DID YOU HEAR ABOUT THE KID WHO SAT UP ALL NIGHT WONDERING WHERE THE SUN HAD GONE?

The next morning it dawned on him.

184

DID YOU HEAR ABOUT THE NIGHT-OWL WHO INSTALLED A SKYLIGHT SO HE COULD WATCH THE STARS?

The people in the room above were furious.

HOW DID THE DOG GET INTO THE LOCKED CEMETERY AT NIGHT?

He used a skeleton key.

IF WE BREATHE OXYGEN IN THE DAYTIME, WHAT DO WE BREATHE AT NIGHT?

Nitrogen!

DID YOU HEAR ABOUT THE WOLVES ALL-NIGHT PARTY?

It was a howling success.

DOCTOR, I HAVE TROUBLE GETTING TO SLEEP AT NIGHT.

Lie on the edge of the bed - you'll soon drop off.

HOW CAN YOU GO WITHOUT SLEEP FOR SEVEN DAYS AND NOT BE TIRED?

Sleep at night.

I'VE BEEN ON MY COMPUTER ALL NIGHT!
Don't you think you'd be more comfortable on a bed like everyone else?

WHAT DANCE CAN YOU SEE IN THE NIGHT SKY?
The Moon Walk.

HOW DOES THE MOON CUT HIS HAIR?
E-clipse it!

WHAT DID MRS. WOLF SAY TO MR. WOLF?
The baby's howling again.

187

WHAT DID ONE BAT SAY TO ANOTHER?

Let's hang around.

WHAT DID ONE GLOW-WORM SAY TO THE OTHER WHEN HIS LIGHT WENT OUT?

Give me a push, my battery is dead.

WHAT DO YOU CALL A DINOSAUR THAT KEEPS YOU AWAKE AT NIGHT?

Bronto-snore-us.

WHAT DO BATS DO AT NIGHT?

Aerobatics.

WHAT DO CALL A CLEVER GLOW-WORM?

A bright spark.

WHAT FISH SWIMS ONLY AT NIGHT?

A starfish.

WHAT GAME DO CATS PLAY AT NIGHT?

Trivial Purr-Suit.

WHAT HOLDS THE MOON UP?

Moon beams.

WHAT IS AN ASTRONOMER?
A night watchman with a college education.

WHAT IS FARTHER AWAY, AUSTRALIA OR THE MOON?
Australia, you can see the moon at night.

WHAT IS THERE MORE OF, THE LESS YOU SEE?
Darkness.

WHAT KIND OF CAR DO WOLVES DRIVE?
A Wolfswagen.

WHAT'S BIG AND BRIGHT AND SILLY?

A fool moon.

WHEN DOES A BED GROW LONGER?

At night, because two feet are added to it.

WHEN IS THE MOON HEAVIEST?

When it's full.

WHICH STARS GO TO JAIL?

Shooting stars.

WHY CAN'T IT RAIN FOR TWO NIGHTS IN A ROW?

Because there is a day in between.

WHY DID YOUR BROTHER GO TO NIGHT SCHOOL?

Because he wanted to learn to read in the dark!

WHY DID THE MAN TAKE A BAG OF OATS TO BED AT NIGHT?

To feed his nightmares.